Out There?

MYSTERIOUS VISITORS

John Townsend

www.raintreepublishers.co.uk

Visit our website to find out more information about **Raintree** books.

To order:
- ☎ Phone 44 (0) 1865 888113
- 📄 Send a fax to 44 (0) 1865 314091
- 💻 Visit the Raintree Bookshop at **www.raintreepublishers.co.uk** to browse our catalogue and order online.

First published in Great Britain by Raintree Publishers, Halley Court, Jordan Hill, Oxford OX2 8EJ, part of Harcourt Education Ltd. Raintree is a registered trademark of Harcourt Education Ltd.

© Harcourt Education Ltd 2004
First published in paperback in 2005.
The moral right of the proprietor has been asserted.

Editorial: Charlotte Guillain and Isabel Thomas
Design: Michelle Lisseter and Bridge Creative Services Ltd
Picture Research: Maria Joannou and Kay Altwegg
Production: Jonathan Smith

Originated by Ambassador
Printed and bound in China

ISBN 1 844 43217 3 (hardback)
08 07 06 05 04
10 9 8 7 6 5 4 3 2 1

ISBN 1 844 43227 0 (paperback)
09 08 07 06 05
10 9 8 7 6 5 4 3 2 1

British Library Cataloguing in Publication Data
Townsend, John, 1924
Mysterious visitors – (Out there)
1. Unidentified flying objects – Juvenile literature
2. Human-alien encounters – Juvenile literature
001.9'42

A full catalogue record for this book is available from the British Library.

Acknowledgements
Page 04–05, Fortean Picture Library/Derek Stafford; 06–07, Corbis/; 06, Fortean Picture Library/; 07, Ronald Grant Archive/; 08–09, Ronald Grant Archive/; 08, Zefa/; 09, Fortean Picture Library/Adam Hart-Davis; 10–11, Science Photo Libray/Simon Fraser; 10, Fortean Picture Library/Marina Jackson; 12–13, Corbis/Steve McDonough; 13, Corbis/Colin Garratt; 14–15, Lonely Planet/Greg Elms; 15, Topham Picturepoint/Performing Arts Library/Pete Jones; 16 right, Fortean Picture Library/; 16 left, Mary Evans Picture Library/; 17, Corbis/Hulton; 18–19, Fortean Picture Library/; 18, Fortean Picture Library/Derek Stafford; 19, Fortean Picture Library/; 20–21, Corbis/; 20, Fortean Picture Library/; 21, Ronal Grant Archive/; 22, Corbis/; 24–25, Corbis/; 24, Corbis/Bill Stormont; 26–27, Constructions Photos/; 26, Corbis/Pawel Libera; 28 bottom, Getty Images/; 28 top, Australian Picture Library/State Library of Victoria; 29, Corbis/Jim Richardson; 30, Corbis/Bettmann; 31, /Tudor photography; 33 left, Fortean Picture Library/; 33, Fortean Picture Library/; 34–35, Corbis/Michael S Yamashita; 34, Corbis/Dave G Houser; 35, Corbis/Lee Snider; 36, Fortean Picture Library/; 37, Fortean Picture Library/; 38 right, Corbis/; 38 left, Corbis/The Corcoran Gallery; 39, Mary Evans Picture Library/; 40 right, Corbis/; 40 left, Corbis/Gustavo Tomsich; 41, Corbis/Adam Woolfitt; 42–43, Corbis/Paul A. Souders; 42, Topham Picturepoint/; 44–45, Aviation Images/; 44, John Frost Newspapers/; 45, Fortean Picture Library/; 46 right, Fortean Picture Library/; 46 left, Fortean Picture Library/Dr Elmar R. Gruber; 47, Getty Images Imagebank/; 48–49, Corbis/Pierre Perrin; 48, Corbis/Pierre Perrin; 49, Fortean Picture Library/; 50–51, Corbis/Todd A Gipstein; 50, Fortean Picture Library/K. F. Lord; 51, Ronald Grant Archive/. Cover photograph reproduced with permission of Topham Picturepoint.

CONTENTS

Any words appearing in the text in bold, **like this**, are explained in the Glossary. You can also look out for them in the Weird words box at the bottom of each page.

MYSTERIOUS MEETINGS

OLD BELIEFS

There are reports of people seeing ghosts in every part of the world. Most cultures and religions believe in some sort of an **afterlife**. Meetings with ghosts were recorded in the Bible, the Koran and in **ancient** Greek and Roman writing. Ghosts have been around for a long time.

You are sitting alone in a room late at night. Suddenly the lights flicker and footsteps creak on the stairs. A door swings open with a gust of icy air. You cannot see anything but you feel a chill run down your back. There is a strange **presence** in the room. You can only croak three words into the darkness: 'Is anybody there?' These are the same three words people have always asked. Ever since they first felt a mysterious visitor in the room.

People have always told ghost stories. Most of us love to hear them. We enjoy a tingle of surprise, of shock, or even of fear. We especially love the fear of the unknown.

Graveyards are often the scene of ghost stories. **>>**

WEIRD WORDS

afterlife   life after death
ancient   from a past age long ago

THE SUPERNATURAL

You are at a wedding and take a picture of the happy couple. But when you get the photos back, you see a strange image between the bride and groom. It is the face of an old uncle who died years ago. Scary? Perhaps there is a simple **explanation**. But often we see or feel things we cannot explain. We just sense that something or someone is there.

People have always asked three big questions:
- Are there such things as ghosts?
- Are there 'unseen powers' out there?
- Is death the end?

And as for the question 'Is anybody there?' – read on to find out if there is an answer.

FIND OUT LATER...

What are 'ghostly visitors' of the first kind?

What are 'ghostly visitors' of the second kind?

Which 'ghostly visitors' cannot be explained?

explanation   reason that can be easily understood
presence   something very near

GHOSTS

- Most religions believe our spirits live on after death.
- For thousands of years people have reported seeing ghosts.
- Halloween, on 31 October, is the night of the year when the dead are said to return to the Earth.

What does a ghost look like? Ask any small child and he or she will describe someone in a white sheet saying 'Oooo'. That is what ghosts look like at Halloween or in cartoons. But is that what they are really like?

WHAT ARE GHOSTS?

It may be best to think of ghosts as 'an unexplained **presence**'. After all, sometimes there is nothing to be seen at all. A strange presence may be a light, a noise or a shape. Sometimes a room fills with a mist, a smell or a sound. Perhaps you feel a shiver or an icy touch. Or it might be a warm breath on the back of your neck...

Not all ghosts are scary!

Most people think of ghosts like this.

WEIRD WORDS   evidence   information available to help prove if something is true or false

FEAR

Ghosts should not really worry us. Despite all the horror films, there are not many stories of ghosts hurting people. We usually find the thought of ghosts scary because we cannot explain what is going on.

When it comes to mysterious visitors:

- Ghosts tend to appear to some people more than to others.
- Ghosts may be linked to **tragic** events. They are like a 'sad shadow left behind'.
- Ghosts are blamed for all sorts of strange events when there is often another **explanation**.
- At times, people can imagine all sorts of things that are not really there.

All you can do is look at the **evidence** and make up your own mind.

ENTERTAINING GHOSTS

Ghosts have appeared in books and plays for hundreds of years. Comic books and films about Casper the Friendly Ghost have been **popular** for over 60 years. The 1995 film *Casper* is about a dead boy who falls in love with a real live girl. Scary and fun!

Casper is known as the Friendly Ghost.

popular   liked by many people
tragic   sad and terrible, with an unhappy ending

NEGATIVE ENERGY

Some people say a poltergeist will move on after:

- a good clean and polish through the house
- a prayer
- oils are burned to clear the room
- salt is sprinkled in every room and left for 24 hours
- **scented** candles are lit in the house.

Poltergeists can actually make things move – even people!

THINGS THAT GO BUMP IN THE NIGHT

In the middle of the night a door creaks open and something bumps down the stairs. There is a thud from the attic and a lamp tips over for no reason. A book sails across the room, but nobody threw it. A table rises up in the air all by itself and plates fall. A door handle turns and a drawer opens...

Some people say these events happen to them most nights. They do not just live in old castles but in new houses and flats as well. Many people learn to live with these bumps in the night, but others say they have simply told 'the visitor' to leave and it has gone.

WEIRD WORDS   disturb   to break the calm and quiet
eerie   weird and frightening

POLTERGEIST

Poltergeist is a German word for 'noisy ghost'. It describes more than a **presence**. These ghosts are said to **disturb** the house with noise. Sometimes they throw objects or push people. A poltergeist does not seem to last in one place for more than three to six months. It may follow just one person in the home. It is almost as if the ghost is trying to tease that person.

Many horror films tell the stories of strange poltergeists. Film makers seem to like this subject because of all the special effects they can use, rather than anything based on fact. Hollywood loves an unseen scary ghost.

RELAX!

Noises in the night are just like noises in the day. They just *seem* more scary. The bumps we hear could just be:

- pets on the move
- floorboards cooling and creaking
- bathroom pipes gurgling
- doors moving in a draught.

Hopefully they are not made by burglars!

A German solicitor made this film of his office lamp swinging. He believed there was a poltergeist in the room.

---

poltergeist   noisy ghost that moves and drops objects
scented   has a pleasant smell

SIGHTINGS

BABY SIGHTING

In 1991 two-year-old Greg Sheldon Maxwell began to say 'Old Nanna's here' and he pointed up in the air. How strange that he should think his dead great-grandmother was in the room. It was even stranger when this weird photograph was developed.

In the 19th century in North Carolina, USA, a boy called Jim Stratton fell in love with Mary Robinson. He was seventeen and she was fifteen. Mary's father wanted to split them up so Jim and Mary ran away into the **bleak** Pisgah Mountains.

LOST LOVERS IN THE SNOW

That night there was a terrible snowstorm. It was the coldest night of the year and the couple must have frozen to death. Jim and Mary were never seen alive again. Every year since then, when the first snow falls, people have seen a ghostly young man kneeling at the feet of a girl in the mountains.

Is Greg looking at the ghost of his great-grandmother?

bleak   bare, cold and windy
blizzard   bad snowstorm

LOST TRAVELLERS IN THE SNOW

Esau Dillingham lived in Labrador, Canada. Between 1910 and 1920 he rode round on a **sled** pulled by his white dogs. He made and sold whisky, which was against the law. This got him into a fight and he broke his back. As he was dying, he prayed, 'Do not send me to hell. Let me drive across this land to undo the wrongs I've done.'

In 1949, two men were lost in a **blizzard**. Suddenly a figure dressed in white fur came through the snow and led the men for miles to a safe hut. They later heard that their guide had been Esau, who had been dead for almost 30 years.

TYPES OF PRESENCE

There are two main types of 'ghostly encounter':

1. Ghostly visitor of the first kind – when people see, hear or sense a ghost or its effects.
2. Ghostly visitor of the second kind – when the ghost makes direct contact and communicates with someone.

Many people have reported seeing ghostly shapes in snowstorms. ««

effect   something that happens as the result of an event or encounter
encounter   unexpected meeting

NEW YORK GHOST TRAIN

A US **legend** tells of the ghostly funeral train that carried President Lincoln's body. It still rumbles along the railway track each April in New York State, more than 100 years after the president's death. Skeletons play in a band on one of the wagons.

GHOST TRAINS

London's underground railway stations can be scary places when no one is about. Aldgate Station has had many scares late at night. At Aldgate, the railway line crosses over very old rails, where strange things happen. These weird events have been recorded in the station **logbook**. People often report distant footsteps drifting down the tunnels in the early hours of the morning. But when anyone goes to look, the footsteps pass by, with no sign of anyone. People have also heard the strange whistling of a ghostly tune in the tunnels late at night. But the **phantom** whistler is never anywhere to be seen.

The tunnels of the London underground may be full of ghosts.

legend   story based on possible grains of truth
logbook   where detailed records of events are written

GHOST OF THE RAILS

Soon after World War Two, a workman was fixing rails deep down in London's underground railway. Repair work was done late at night, when the trains had stopped running. A driver saw the workman on the track. Suddenly an old woman with white hair appeared. The driver saw her gently stroking the back of the workman's head. Just then the railway worker made a horrible mistake. He touched the deadly 24,000-volt electric rail. The sudden shock knocked him out but, strangely, he was unharmed.

People think the old woman had been killed when she fell on to the rail during the bombing of London in World War Two.

THE GHOST TRAIN OF ST LOUIS

Another legend tells of a railway conductor who was inspecting the track in St Louis, USA, when a train chopped off his head. Even though the track was taken up years ago, lights and the sound of steam still fill the night.

Locals say they have often met the St Louis ghost train. >>

UNIVERSITY OF NORTH IOWA THEATRE

The theatre at North Iowa University, USA has a ghost called Zelda. One night when the theatre was full, an electric cable fell onto the only empty seat. People think Zelda guided it so no one was hurt. She also opens doors, swears, plays the piano and cries like a baby.

GHOSTS ON STAGE

Theatres all over the world are supposed to be haunted by ghosts. Maybe it is because theatres are dark places or because actors are **superstitious**. Whatever the reason, many theatres have their own ghost stories.

MELBOURNE

The Princess Theatre in Melbourne, Australia is the home to a ghost called Federici. He was an English singer whose real name was Fred Baker. He died of a heart attack in the middle of a play as he was going down through a **trapdoor**. Since that night in 1888, Federici has visited plays at the theatre. He is a smart ghost and always wears a black suit. Superstitious actors like to think he is a sign of good luck.

Some theatres, such as the Princess Theatre in Melbourne, are supposed to have their own ghosts. ➤➤

WEIRD WORDS

rehearsal   practise for a performance
superstitious   believing in luck and the supernatural

THEATRE ROYAL, DRURY LANE

The Theatre Royal in Drury Lane is the oldest theatre in London. It was built in 1663 and it is supposed to be haunted. One of its ghosts is the Man in Grey. He wears a long grey coat and a white wig, and he carries a sword. He looks like he is from the 18th century and he watches plays from the balcony. Then he disappears into the wall. He is usually around between 9 a.m. and 6 p.m., so he often pops up at **rehearsals**. Actors think it is lucky to see the Man in Grey.

Another ghost is said to give actresses a friendly pat on the back before they go on stage.

THE EMPRESS THEATRE

At the Empress Theatre in Fort Mcleod, Canada, there is a ghost called Ed. He is friendly, apart from when he throws rubbish from the bins. He sits in the balcony during shows, moves coffee cups and sometimes cries in the dressing room. He has even helped to sell tickets.

Other theatres have to make do with actors playing ghosts on stage.

IMAGE ON THE STAIRS

The stairs of the Naval College in London are home to a hooded figure. No one knows who he is. A photo was taken of the ghost in 1966 and it does not seem to be a **hoax**. So who is the sad figure, with a ring on his right hand?

THE BROWN LADY OF RAYNHAM HALL

In 1936, two men went to Raynham Hall, a grand house in Norfolk, England. They wanted a photo of the fine hallway for the cover of a magazine. One of them saw a strange shadow on the stairs and screamed for the other to take a picture. The result is the well-known photo of the 'Brown Lady' ghost.

This photo of the Brown Lady may be a hoax.

Ghosts are often seen and even photographed on staircases. Is it just a trick of the light?

hoax   not real, a joke

DOROTHY

Is the Brown Lady the ghost of Dorothy Walpole? Dorothy's brother was one of England's prime ministers. She married the owner of Raynham Hall in 1712. Her husband locked her in her room at the Hall but nobody knows why. She died unhappy. Perhaps she had smallpox or maybe her husband murdered her.

SHOT

In 250 years, the Brown Lady has appeared many times. Her portrait was in one of the most haunted rooms of the house. Two boys saw a tall lady with a **lantern** float across the hallway towards them. They froze and watched as she drifted past. Then she turned and glared at them with a look full of hate.

In 1844, one man was so scared when he saw the Brown Lady that he shot at her. The bullet went right through her and at that moment she disappeared. She was not seen again for nearly half a century. So when will she next drift down those haunted stairs?

GHOST LIGHTS

At Silver Cliff, Colorado, in the USA, people have seen dancing lights in the graveyard at night. Are they the helmet lamps of ghost miners coming up the steps of the old silver mine? Are they the dancing spirits of Native Americans buried here? Or is there another **explanation**?

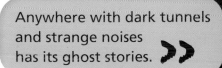

Anywhere with dark tunnels and strange noises has its ghost stories. ≫

HAUNTED CHURCHYARD

One of the most haunted villages in England is said to be Prestbury in Gloucestershire. This is because many houses have ghosts and so does the church. In 1990, Derek Stafford took photos of the **floodlit** churchyard. He found a hooded 'Black Abbot' on his last photo.

THE MOVING COFFINS OF BARBADOS

It was the custom 200 years ago for rich people in the West Indies to have a family **vault** at the local church. This was often **bricked up** again after each new coffin was put inside. It would normally be many years between each 'opening' of the vault.

In Barbados between 1812 and 1820, there was a mysterious family vault with six coffins inside, all placed in order. The door to the vault was sealed with a large marble slab. It took at least four men to open up the door. But each time the vault was opened up, all the coffins inside had moved. They were all mixed up.

Derek Stafford's famous photo of the Black Abbot. **>>**

brick up   to close or block with bricks
floodlit   to be lit up by large, powerful lights

JUMBLED

Over eight years, the vault was opened five times. Each time, the coffins had moved again. There were no marks in the sand on the floor. There were no signs of water or footprints. It looked like the heavy coffins had been thrown all over the place. How it happened remains a mystery to this day.

In the end, the family took the coffins out of the vault and buried them in separate graves. The story of the moving coffins became a famous **legend** of the West Indies.

SS WATERTOWN

Two sailors were cleaning the oil tank of the SS *Watertown* as it sailed from New York in 1924. They were killed by **gas fumes** and their bodies were buried at sea. The next day, the sailors' ghostly faces appeared on the water behind the ship.

The entrance to a family vault in Barbados where strange things happened.

These phantom faces followed the SS *Watertown* for days.

gas fumes   harmful vapour from chemicals
vault   room for storing coffins

MAKING CONTACT

People used to bury bodies at crossroads. This was thought to confuse ghosts who would not know which way to leave. They would then have to stay at their resting place. A lot of criminals were hung from trees next to crossroads for this reason.

Ghosts may do more than just appear. They may make things happen.

There are stories of murder **victims** coming back to haunt their killers. It is not just for **revenge** – the ghost may want the police to know what happened to them.

THE VICTIM RETURNS

Teresita Basa was a nurse in Chicago, USA. She was stabbed to death in her apartment in 1977. Her jewels were missing, but there was no sign of a break-in. Police thought Teresita must have known her killer and let him in. But they had no clues at all. Remy was Teresita's friend. She saw Teresita's ghost. Then she dreamed she saw Teresita talking to a strange man.

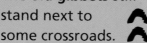
The old **gibbets** still stand next to some crossroads.

gibbet   pole for hanging criminals
jury   group of people who decide if a person is guilty

THE SUSPECT

One day Remy saw the man from her dream. His name was Al Showery and it turned out he had known Teresita. Remy was sure he was the killer, but how could she prove it?

Remy told the police. Al said he had agreed to fix Teresita's TV but that he never went to her house. The police spoke to Al's girlfriend. She wore a ring that Al had given her.

Teresita's ghost returned. It told Remy to call Teresita's cousin, who said, 'That's Teresita's ring!' Had Al murdered Teresita and stolen the ring? The police and **jury** thought so. Al went to prison for 22 years. Teresita's ghost had won the case.

DVD GHOSTS

Spooky old houses with closed, heavy curtains and flickering candles have been part of ghost films for years. *The Others*, starring Nicole Kidman, is set in 1945 in a scary house. The **tension** grows as something seems to be making contact...

The Others is a ghost film with a twist.

tension   mental strain and excitement
victim   person who gets hurt or killed

HAUNTED HOUSE OF CRYSTAL LAKE, ILLINOIS, USA

George Stickney built Stickney **Mansion** in 1849 without many corners to the rooms. He believed ghosts could hide in corners. George Stickney was found dead in the only **right-angled** corner in the house with a frozen, terrified look on his face. His hands were clutching at his throat. How he died remains a mystery.

THE HANDS OF DEATH

Motorbike riders on a road in Devon, England, have felt hairy hands suddenly grab their handlebars. At least two riders have been thrown off their bikes. One said, 'I saw a hairy hand touch the handlebars just before I went off the road.'

HAUNTED ROAD

On another English country road, 20 cars crashed into the same hedge in 2002. The drivers said their steering wheels were pulled from their hands. Local people at Stoke Lacey said a girl in a black Ford died at the same spot in the 1940s. Just before she crashed, she was seen fighting with a man at the wheel.

> George Stickney believed that no corners meant no ghosts!

mansion   very large house
right-angled   90° angle

PHANTOM HITCHHIKER

Mae Doria was driving on Highway 20 in Tulsa, Oklahoma, USA in 1965. She saw a hand waving ahead so she slowed down to see who it was. It was a boy of about 12 years old, hitchhiking. Mae thought he was too young to be out on such a cold night so she offered him a ride. The boy got into the car and chatted about basketball. Then he said, 'Can you let me out here?' Mae looked hard to see where the boy meant and turned to ask him. But suddenly, he vanished. Mae stopped the car and ran around looking for the boy. He was nowhere to be seen.

"

I was in a caravan on a moonlit night. My husband was asleep by the window. Suddenly a very large hairy hand came clawing at the open window. I knew it wished to harm my husband. I prayed and the hand sank out of sight.'

"

Written by a woman from Devon in 1923.

These ghostly hands have thrown riders off their motorbikes in Devon, England. ‹‹

TENNESSEE MYSTERY

John Bell Junior kept his father's farm going until he died in 1862. The house stood for many years but was burned down in the early part of the 20th century. Some people believe the Bell Witch ghost may have started the flames.

THE BELL WITCH

John Bell and his family lived in a **remote** farmhouse in Robertson County, Tennessee in the USA. From 1817, the house seemed to have a **poltergeist**. There were odd noises in the night. All five of John's children had their faces slapped by unseen hands. Betsy, his 12-year-old daughter, had the worst of it. She heard frightening voices. The family thought the strange visitor was the ghost of some sort of witch.

Hardly a night passed in three years without the 'witch' yelling. The strain was too much for John Bell. He became ill and weak, and on the morning of 20 December 1820, he died.

Can ghosts start fires?

remote   far away from other people

THE BOTTLE

After John's death, the family found a small bottle of liquid. John had drunk it the night before he died. His son, John Bell Junior, picked up the bottle. The ghost suddenly spoke again: 'I gave John Bell a big dose of that last night, and that fixed him.' John Junior threw the bottle into the fireplace. It shot up the chimney in a bright blue flame.

After a few more months of **shrieks** in the night, the haunting stopped at last. All that was left was the **legend** of the Bell Witch. Some people still sense a **presence** in the field where the Bell's house once stood.

BOOKS ON THE BELL WITCH HAUNTING

The full story is told in many books...

Even now, many people still have strange **encounters** near the old Bell farm. They tell of the sounds of **phantom** children playing in a cave, and the appearance of a young woman floating just above the ground.

Ghost stories are often set in remote places like this old farmhouse. Are there really more ghosts, or are people just more easily scared? **‹‹**

shriek   shrill screech

MYSTERY WITH A BIT OF MISCHIEF – GHOSTS WHO INTERFERE

- A poltergeist smashed so many cups in a china shop in Miami, USA in 1967 that the police came to arrest it.

- The ghost jockey Fred Archer rides the racecourse at Newmarket, England, and frightens horses.

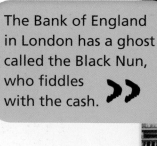

The Bank of England in London has a ghost called the Black Nun, who fiddles with the cash.

PLAYING TRICKS

It seems some ghosts like to **interfere**. They enjoy giving people a hard time. Sometimes ghosts are said to cause trouble in the most ordinary houses.

ENFIELD, LONDON

In 1977, a **poltergeist** was blamed for strange things in a small council house in Enfield, London. Two children called Janet and Peter lived in the house. One night they screamed that their beds were moving. When their mother ran into the room, nothing happened. She was sure the children were just joking. Then there were four loud knocks on the wall. A heavy chest of drawers began moving across the floor. Their mother tried to push it back but it would not move.

infrared   the wavelength of light that allows a camera to 'see in the dark'

FAMOUS

On 10 September 1977, the Enfield story made the front page of the *Daily Mirror*. Lots of people came to **investigate** the 'visitor'. Anything electrical would stop or splutter. Batteries seemed to drain of power. An **infrared** television camera brought to film the bedroom broke down.

Experts thought there was a strange energy in the house. But others thought it was the children who were making the mischief. Janet said she floated about the room. Then people heard her talking in strange voices. She went away for tests and the house calmed down. The family moved to another house and the trouble stopped. Their old house was quiet again.

GHOST SHIP

One Dutch **legend** tells of a **phantom** boat that ferries dead souls across the sea from The Netherlands to Britain. This tale was told to explain why the UK has so many ghosts compared with the rest of Europe.

It seems that a house does not have to be old to have a ghost.

interfere   meddle and get in the way
investigate   search and study very carefully

GHOSTLY PLACES

MURDER

The most recent death at Monte Cristo was in 1961. The caretaker, Jack Simpson was murdered. After watching a horror film, a local boy made his way up to the grounds of the house with a rifle and shot Jack dead in his cottage. Some think Jack's ghost still returns.

Monte Cristo is a house of mystery in the town of Junee, Australia. Mr Crawley built the house in 1884 and lived there with his bossy wife for 25 years. She lived there alone after his death. She never left the house, until she died in 1933. After she died the house stayed empty and fell into ruin. Nobody **restored** Monte Cristo or lived in it again until 1961.

CHILLING

The house and grounds are now said to have at least seven ghosts. Mrs Crawley's ghost has been heard to order people out of the dining room. The people who live there now feel her **presence** when a room suddenly goes icy cold.

Floating faces are said to peer in through the upstairs windows of Monte Cristo! **>>**

WEIRD WORDS

coach house   building where carriages were kept
peer   look keenly but with some difficulty

WOULD YOU DARE SPEND THE NIGHT IN MONTE CRISTO?

- **M**eet the maid from years ago who fell to her death from upstairs. The blood-stained steps below were scrubbed but the bleach marks remain. Her ghost is thought to return to this day, maybe still scrubbing the steps!

- **H**ear footsteps walking through empty rooms. The hall and the stairs echo with weird noises. Hollow footsteps sound as though someone is walking on hard floors even though the house now has carpets.

- **S**ee faces peering in through upstairs windows, or vases moving around the drawing room. And why does the wall tapestry often lie on the floor in the morning?

WOULD **YOU** SLEEP IN A HOUSE LIKE THIS?

THE GROUNDS OF MONTE CRISTO

The **coach house** in the grounds of Monte Cristo was where a stable boy named Morris slept. The story says he was ill one morning. His cruel boss did not believe him and set fire to his bedding. Morris was burned to death and it is said his ghost returns.

Monte Cristo House has many ghostly mysteries.

restore   repair and bring back something to its original state

CHALLENGE

Ghosts were big business and tourists were ready to pay.

BEST SELLER

A best-selling book about a haunted house came out in 1977. It shocked the world. Could ghosts really be so terrible? Then a film was made of the story and it made a fortune. People were gripped by this 'true story of a family's terror'. But was the story true or were people just **conned**?

AMITYVILLE

The famous house was in Amityville, Long Island, New York. The true horror was in 1974 when Ronald DeFeo killed his parents, two brothers and two sisters in the house. He was 23. He told the court that a ghost in the house made him do it. He was sent to prison for life.

Ronald DeFeo claimed a ghost made him kill his family in this house. But the court did not believe in ghosts.

con   fool, trick and generally 'take-in'

FROM BAD TO WORSE

Then the Lutz family moved into the house. They only stayed one month. They could stand it no longer, or so they said. George Lutz told of terrible things in the house. Red eyes stared in through windows and green slime oozed from keyholes. Hooded figures, clouds of flies, icy chills, sickly smells and moving objects happened most nights. George Lutz said the house was evil.

FAME

The press and TV rushed to the house. The world soon knew of The Amityville Horror. Ghosts became big news and many people got rich. Years later, George Lutz's story and the famous book were seen to be a huge **hoax**.

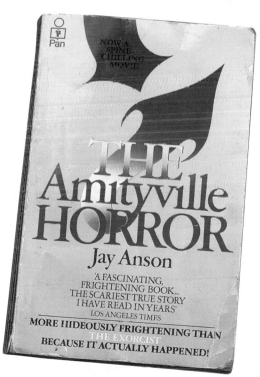

THE LAST MYSTERIOUS CHAPTER

- Jay Anson wrote the best selling book *The Amityville Horror*. He died just after he got a million dollar deal for his next book.

- Another writer of the Amityville story died suddenly.

- Stephen Kaplan wrote a book about the Amityville hoax. He died before it was published.

Could the Amityville Horror be the most **jinxed** story ever? Jay Anson died soon after writing this book. **‹‹**

FOUNDATIONS

A new vicar came to the village of Borley in 1863. Henry Bull and his wife wanted a big house for their fourteen children. He built a red-brick house on a plot of land. Unknown to him, a body lay buried on the land.

This photo of ghostly scribbles on the walls of Borley Rectory was taken by investigators.

THE CHURCH HOUSE

Borley is 60 miles north-east of London. The village **rectory** was built in 1863 on the site of a **convent**. It soon became known as the most haunted house in England.

An old **legend** told of a monk who fell in love with one of the nuns at the convent. They were about to run away together but were caught. The monk was hanged and the nun was **bricked up** alive in the cellar of the convent.

NOISES IN THE NIGHT

Around 1900, people began to notice strange things about the house. There were odd noises. A nun kept appearing in the garden. Locals said the place was haunted.

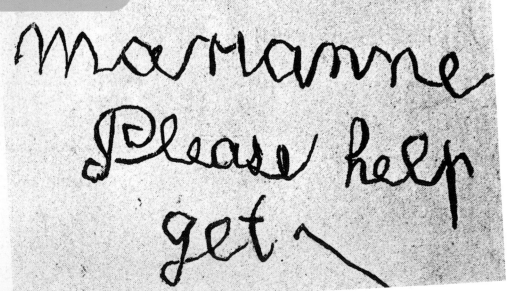

convent   home for nuns
rectory   house of the vicar of the local church

THE NUN RETURNS

Until the 1930s, different families who lived in the house told stories of whispers in the night. There were ghostly footsteps, objects thrown at guests and strange lights. Two maids saw the nun many times, as well as a **phantom** coach on the drive.

FIRE

Marianne was the wife of the **vicar** who lived in the house. She was hit in the face and flung from her bed. Something wrote her name on the walls.

In 1939, more writing appeared. A message warned that the house would burn down that night. Nothing happened. But a few months later the house caught fire at midnight. By the morning it was no more than a ruin.

AFTER THE FIRE

Far below Borley Rectory's ashes was an old cellar. Bricked up inside was a skeleton of a young woman. Maybe she was the nun whose sad ghost walked the grounds. New houses now stand on the spot, but people sometimes see a nun in the gardens, still trying to find rest...

Borley Rectory was in ruins after the fire.

PORT ARTHUR, TASMANIA

In the 19th century, prisoners were shipped to Port Arthur Prison from Britain – sometimes just for stealing food or clothes. Being sent to Port Arthur was a nightmare. It had the name 'Hell On Earth'. Even if prisoners were let out, they would never be able to pay their fare home.

HAUNTED PRISONS

Many old prisons were places of **despair**. Even now they seem to cry with the pain of **lost souls**.

100 GHOSTS OF ALCATRAZ

In the prison on Alactraz Island, USA, men slept side by side on stone floors. The prison closed in 1963 after a hundred years of misery, but its many ghosts are still said to drift round the cells. People have heard clanging, screams, crying and someone playing a banjo. Once a violent killer called The Butcher was murdered by another prisoner. Now The Butcher's angry ghost is meant to roar his plan of **revenge**.

Feelings of evil and hatred still seem to **lurk** in the shadows at the dreaded Alcatraz.

A prisoner's first view of the guard tower at Port Arthur.

convict   to find guilty of a crime and send to prison
despair   complete loss of hope

MAITLAND PRISON

Maitland was another harsh prison, about 160 kilometres (100 miles) from Sydney in Australia. It was still open and in use until January 1998. It was one of the toughest prisons in Australia.

Today, Maitland is known as one of Australia's most haunted sites open to the public. Dark figures are said to wander around the cells at night. They grab, scratch and push visitors or breathe down their necks. Ghostly sights appear and strange noises echo round the passages. Guides who take the night tours have felt many mysterious **presences**. Misery from the past still seems to haunt the thick cold walls.

BURLINGTON PRISON, NEW JERSEY, USA

Burlington Prison closed in 1966. For years people told of the ghost of Joseph Clough, a **convicted** murderer. He had been chained in a **death row** cell until he was hanged in the 1850s. Ever since, guards and prisoners have reported hearing his moans and chains rattling from that cell.

The entrance to Burlington Prison, which is now a museum.

lost soul   sad ghost that cannot find rest after a miserable life
death row   section of a prison for people sentenced to death

DOVER CASTLE

Dover Castle is meant to have many ghosts, but they never appear when people try to take photos of them. A ghost of a woman in a red dress has appeared on the stairs. A **bricked-up** doorway sometimes creaks ... just as if the door is still there.

HAUNTED CASTLES

Like prisons, castles seem to have many restless spirits within their walls. Do **dungeons** and torture leave sad souls behind?

CHILLINGHAM CASTLE – BRITAIN'S MOST HAUNTED CASTLE?

There have been many battles on the borders between Scotland and England. Now this area is a place where ghosts seem to wander. Chillingham Castle's most famous ghost was the '**Radiant** Boy'. On the stroke of midnight he was said to cry in fear. The noises came from the Pink Bedroom through a thick wall. When the cries stopped, a glow would appear around the old four-poster bed. Anyone asleep in the bed would wake up to see a young boy dressed in blue.

Ghosts reported at Dover Castle include Roman soldiers and a headless drummer.

dungeon   dark underground cell for locking up prisoners
footman   servant

MYSTERY BONES

Human remains with bits of blue cloth were found inside the Pink Bedroom's wall. They were the bones of a boy. After they were buried in the nearby churchyard his ghost no longer appeared.

THE LADY IN WHITE

A white figure is still said to appear in the inner **pantry** now and again. One night a **footman** locked himself inside the pantry to guard the silver. He woke up to see a lady in white. She asked him for a glass of water. Thinking she was a guest, he poured her the water and then remembered he had locked himself inside the pantry. How did she get in? He turned to ask, but she had gone.

Glamis castle is just the place for ghost hunting.

GLAMIS CASTLE, SCOTLAND

Shakespeare wrote about Glamis Castle in his play *Macbeth*. He had heard it was full of mystery and hauntings.

- Macbeth may have murdered King Duncan within the castle walls.

- Blood stained the floor so badly that the room was bricked up.

pantry   walk-in food store
radiant   glowing

GHOSTLY PEOPLE

THE PRESIDENT OF THE USA

Abraham Lincoln lived from 1809 to 1865. He became president in 1861. He was known for his loud laugh which some say they still hear today. They also hear ghostly footsteps near his grave in Springfield, Illinois. A **legend** says that the grave is empty.

Some ghosts have names like 'The White Lady' or 'The **Radiant** Boy'. But others have real names and are said to be the ghosts of famous people.

A FAMOUS GHOST

Abraham Lincoln was the sixteenth US president. He was shot dead at a theatre in 1865. Ten days before he died, Lincoln dreamed of his own death. He wrote in his diary:

> I saw a coffin guarded by soldiers. Crowds were crying as they passed the body.
> 'Who is dead in the White House?' I asked.
> 'The President. He was shot.' A cry rose from the crowd and woke me from my dream. It was only a dream yet it has **disturbed** me ever since.

The White House may be haunted by Abraham Lincoln's ghost. **>>**

WEIRD WORDS   distinct   unmistakable
heads of state   leaders of different countries

THE WHITE HOUSE

Lincoln's ghost may haunt the White House. His energy and **distinct** laugh are still felt in the rooms. Staff claim to have seen his dark outline at a window in the Oval Office. Visiting **heads of state** often report strange appearances in his old bedroom, now called the Lincoln Room. Others who lived in the White House said they met the ghost.

- President Roosevelt's wife sensed Lincoln's **presence** late at night.
- Her dog, Fala, would bark for no reason. Perhaps it could sense the ghost.
- President Truman heard Lincoln walking through the house.
- President Reagan's daughter said she saw Lincoln's ghost in the Lincoln Room.

THE BODYGUARD

Lincoln told his bodyguard about his bad dream. The bodyguard begged him not to go to the theatre that night. Lincoln said he must. Maybe he knew he might be shot. The last word he said to the bodyguard was 'goodbye' instead of his usual 'goodnight'.

A painting of the shooting of Lincoln.

MARY QUEEN OF SCOTS

Of all the royal ghosts, the one of Mary Queen of Scots appears in the most places. Mary travelled a lot and stayed in many castles. So does her ghost, apparently.

They say that the ghost of Mary Queen of Scots haunts the wooden staircase in Fotheringhay Castle that she used to walk to her **execution** in 1587.

ROYAL GHOSTS

It seems that kings and queens still like to keep a ghostly eye on things. Many of their ghosts have been seen in palace passages. People say they bump into Henry VIII of England all the time. He appears as a restless ghost. It may be that Henry was a troubled king because he had a lot of people killed.

Henry lived at Hampton Court. In fact, even he used to see ghosts there when he was alive. He was the first to see the headless ghost of his second wife, Anne Boleyn. Henry's ghost is now said to walk through Hampton Court too. Maybe the two ghosts chat about old times.

Do ghosts still walk around the gardens of Hampton Court?

execution   carrying out the sentence of death

HENRY'S QUEENS

- Anne Boleyn was beheaded in the Tower of London so that Henry could marry again. He and others have seen her ghost since – with her head tucked under her arm.

- Jane Seymour was Henry's next queen. She died giving birth to his son Edward. On that date each year, she floats up the stairs at Hampton Court with a candle.

- Henry found out that another wife, Katherine Howard, loved someone else. She begged him not to harm her but he still had her beheaded. Her ghost runs screaming and begging today.

- Henry's daughter, Queen Elizabeth I, seems to pop up quite a lot, too. Her ghost has often been reported at Windsor Castle.

THE TOWER OF LONDON

Anne Boleyn has appeared near the Tower of London where she was beheaded. One night guards saw lights in the chapel. Through a window they saw ghosts in **Tudor** clothes. Anne Boleyn was with them. Then the light faded and the chapel was left in darkness.

Traitors' Gate at the Tower of London was once used by prisoners arriving by boat.

Tudor   period in English history between 1485 and 1603

MARILYN MONROE

Marilyn Monroe was a famous film star who died in 1962. She used to stay at Hollywood's Roosevelt Hotel, where people say they have seen her ghost in a mirror. If her sad **reflection** appears, people turn to see if Marilyn is behind them. Of course, there is nothing there.

FISHER'S GHOST

The story of Fisher's Ghost is now famous in Australia. Fred Fisher's murdered body was found in a field in Campbelltown in 1826. But only after his ghost told a neighbour where to look.

One night, Farmer Farley was sure he saw a ghost sitting on a fence. It was in an **eerie** white light, with blood dripping from its head. The ghost gave a loud moan, raised an arm and pointed to a **creek** on George Worrall's land. Farley went to the police, who found Fred Fisher's remains in the creek. George Worrall turned out to be Fred's killer and was hanged for murder. All because of a ghost.

creek   stream

BLACK AGGIE

Felix Angus was an army general who died in 1925. His family had a statue made for his grave in Baltimore, USA. The statue was a black angel that people called 'Black Aggie'. By day it was an angel but by night it became something more scary. Locals said ghosts gathered when the angel's eyes glowed red on the stroke of midnight. They said that if any human looked into the angel's eyes, they would fall down dead. A young student was found dead beside Black Aggie one morning. People believed he had died of fright.

In 1967 the statue of Black Aggie was sent to a Washington museum and peace returned to the cemetery.

MAD ANTHONY'S GHOST

Anthony Wayne was an army general who died in Pennsylvania, USA in 1796. He was buried in Erie, but his son later wanted his bones moved. The **legend** says that some of Anthony's bones fell from the wagon and now his ghost still madly searches the road for them.

This Australian ghost hunter investigates mysterious sightings and paranormal effects. **‹‹**

reflection   image seen in a mirror

Evening News

Helicopter nets scoop up survivors from TriStar disaster

GIANT JET CRASHES IN SWAMP: 80 DIE

MIAMI, Saturday.
A GIANT TRISTAR jet with 167 people on board crashed early today in the Everglades swamp. At least 80 passengers and crew were killed.

The newspaper report of the crash.

> " There was ripping and tearing and people crying. I thought I was in a dream. I was just turning, twisting, everything happening at once. It wasn't like people say, your life passing before you. There wasn't any warning. It just happened. "
>
> Jerry Solomon, survivor of Flight 401.

FLIGHT 401

Bob Loft and Don Repo were pilots flying from New York to Miami in 1977. Just as they got close to landing they lost control of the plane. They fought to keep Flight 401 in the air but they failed. Both men died, as well as around 80 passengers.

PILOTS RETURN

Three months after the crash, pilots said Loft and Repo appeared in their planes. Other staff began to report seeing the two men on different flights. A passenger saw a pale man in uniform in the seat next to her. She asked a flight attendant if he was well and with that, the ghostly figure disappeared in full view of everyone. The woman screamed.

wreckage   smashed remains after a crash

WARNING

When she was shown photos of Eastern Airlines staff, the trembling passenger picked out Don Repo as the man she had seen sitting next to her.

A flight attendant on another flight opened an oven door and was shocked to see Repo's face looking out. She screamed and fetched two other staff. One had been Repo's friend and recognized him straight away. All three heard Repo warn them to 'Watch out for fire on this airplane'. A few days later, the aircraft lost an engine while taking off from Mexico City. Another engine burst into flames a few minutes later. Luckily the plane landed safely.

The story of Flight 401 was made into a book and film.

SPARE PARTS

After Loft and Repo's plane crashed in 1977, a writer looked into the mysterious appearances. Parts from the plane's **wreckage** were used in other aircraft where the ghosts then seemed to appear. Eastern Airlines replaced the spare parts and the ghosts were no longer seen.

GHOST FAQS

MYSTERY PHOTO

In 1978, on the day after his mother's death, Silvio went for a walk in the woods in Switzerland. He saw a strange light and took this photo. The photo shows a 'ghost like an angel'. Is it a **hoax**, a trick of the light or something more?

There is nothing like a scary tale when you are sitting in the dark. But what are the facts?

ARE THERE ANIMAL GHOSTS?

There are only a few accounts of animal ghosts. Some tell of horses appearing out of the mist. Others tell of mystery black dogs that appear out of nowhere.

A **phantom** dog appeared in a photo in 1926. Lady Hehir had a cairn puppy called Kathal. It died six weeks before she took a photo of her Irish wolfhound. The two dogs had been good friends. Kathal's ghost appears to be there in the photo.

The head of Lady Hehir's dead puppy appeared in this photo of her new dog. **>>**

WHY DO SOME PEOPLE WAKE UP, SEE A GHOST AND CANNOT MOVE?

Maybe they did not really see a ghost. If people sleep with their eyes open, they may 'see things' in their sleep. The imagination can seem very real in some ghostly dreams. People often wake up in a panic and are unable to move for a while.

WHY DO HAUNTINGS ALWAYS TAKE PLACE AT NIGHT?

They do not. People who study ghosts say hauntings can be at all times of the day. Maybe ghosts prefer to visit at night when it is quieter and they are less likely to **disturb** people. So perhaps that is why the night-time is often the best time to go ghost hunting. After all, that is when most strange things seem to happen.

A GOOD PLACE TO SEE A GHOST

Bachelor's Grove Cemetery in the USA is known as one of Chicago's most haunted places. One of its many mysteries is 'Madonna', yet no one knows who she really was. She has been seen carrying a baby on nights with a full moon. When her arms are empty, it is said she is looking for the baby.

Graveyards are spooky places, so it is not surprising that most are said to be haunted. **‹‹**

THE CALIFORNIAN GHOST TOWN

Bodie is said to be the most haunted ghost town in the world. It is now a state park. Once, some rangers threw a rock down an old mine shaft and they heard a ghostly voice yell back from below, 'Hey, You!' Scary.

The ruined buildings at Bodie may hide many secrets.

Is this the most haunted town in the world? >>

WHAT ARE GHOST TOWNS?

An empty town is an **eerie** place. Some ghost towns have been left just as they were. This happened in the Middle Ages if **plague** hit a village. It also happened in gold mining areas if the gold ran out. All that was left was the wind rattling round the empty houses and the ghosts of those who once lived there.

BODIE

In the late 1870s the town of Bodie in California, USA, had a **population** of 10,000 people. It was well known for killings and robberies. There were **hold-ups** and street fights. But then flu and other diseases swept through Bodie. Whole families were wiped out within a week. Today, only the sad ghosts remain.

helmsman   sailor who steers a ship
jealous   full of envy and hate of another person's success

WHAT ARE GHOST SHIPS?

For centuries sailors have told stories of ghostly 'drifters'. These were empty ships that appeared through sea mists only to disappear into thin air again. They were meant to be the ghosts of wrecks now on the seabed.

WATERY GRAVE

In 1748, the captain of the *Lady Lovibond* took 50 guests on the ship for his wedding. The problem was, his **helmsman** was also in love with his bride. While the wedding party was below decks, the **jealous** helmsman steered the ship on to the Goodwin Sands in a rage. Everyone was drowned. Since then, people say they have seen a ghostly ship crashing on to the sand bank in the English Channel and sinking below the icy waves.

The *Flying Dutchman* as seen in 1881.

THE *FLYING DUTCHMAN*

This ghost ship is said to be the curse of the seas. In 1881, people on the *Bacchante* saw the *Flying Dutchman* in a strange red light. Six hours later, the first man to have spotted the ship was killed.

plague   deadly disease that spreads quickly
population   all the people who live in a place or country

DO GHOSTS KEEP AWAY FROM CHURCHES?

Why should they? There are many reports of 'friendly ghosts' popping into church. In fact, a **vicar** took this photo of an altar in the 1960s. When the picture was developed, he saw a mysterious shadow. Is it the hooded figure of a monk?

WHAT SORTS OF HAUNTINGS ARE THERE?

- Some ghostly remains are a bit like a tape recording of a past event. Very strong feelings may leave an **imprint** in time. Some of the energy remains. This could be the sound of somebody falling down the stairs. Or it may be in the form of a blob of light called an **orb**.
- Anniversary ghosts are only meant to visit on special dates – deaths, birthdays and times that hold a meaning. They may **re-enact** a special event.
- An intelligent haunting is when the soul of a dead person is thought to remain on the Earth. Perhaps it still looks for someone to 'talk' to. It can be playful, like a **poltergeist**.

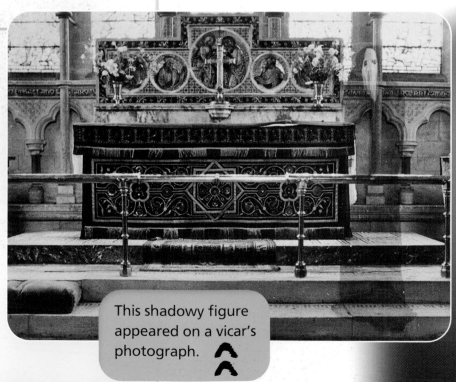

This shadowy figure appeared on a vicar's photograph.

50   **WEIRD WORDS**   imprint   stamp or impression
                          orb   shape of a ball or the globe

MAYBE ... MAYBE NOT...

Many of the mysterious visitors in this book can be explained. Imagination and tricks of the mind can explain a lot. Mistakes, **hoaxes** and confusions account for most. And of course, many people want to believe in ghosts. But ... there always remain real mysteries. Science cannot explain them all. So – is anybody there? In truth, no one can be really sure. In the end, you just have to make up your own mind...

Orbs seen in photos are often formed by dust, mist or tricks of the light.

AND FINALLY ... GHOSTS CAN BE FUN

Scooby Doo is one of the most successful cartoons ever made. The team of four teenagers and Scooby the dog have solved hundreds of ghost mysteries since the cartoon started in 1969.

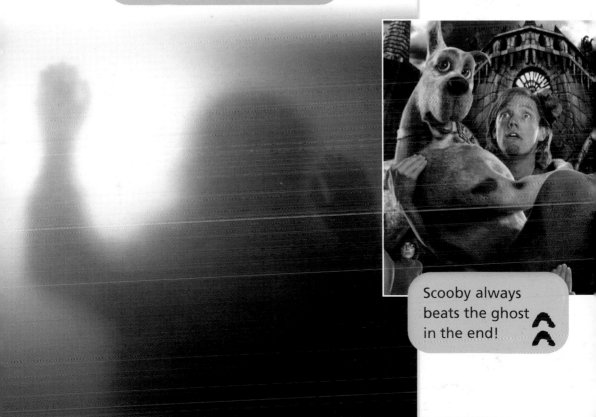

Scooby always beats the ghost in the end!

FIND OUT MORE

GHOSTLY WEBSITES

GHOST MYSTERIES
Online magazine about ghosts and UFOs.
mysterymag.com

GHOST TOWNS
Photos and stories from ghost towns across the USA.
ghosttowngallery.com

BELL WITCH
Website dedicated to this famous ghost story.
bellwitch.org

BOOKS
Can Science Solve? The Mystery of Haunted Houses, Chris Oxlade and Anita Ganeri (Heinemann Library, 2001)
Ghosts: Haunted Houses and Spooky Stories, (Tick Tock, 2002)
The Supernatural, Phenomena Beyond Belief (Tick Tock, 2002)

WORLD WIDE WEB
If you want to find out more about **mysterious visitors**, you can search the Internet using keywords like these:
- 'bell witch'
- 'ghost stories'
- Flight 401 + ghosts
- Hampton Court + ghosts
- Alcatraz prison + ghosts
- [name of your area] + ghosts

You can also find your own keywords by using headings or words from this book. Use the search tips below to help you find the most useful websites.

SEARCH TIPS

There are billions of pages on the Internet so it can be difficult to find exactly what you are looking for. For example, if you just type in 'ghost' on a search engine like Google, you will get a list of 6 million web pages. These search skills will help you find useful websites more quickly:

- Know exactly what you want to find out about first
- Use simple keywords instead of whole sentences
- Use two to six keywords in a search, putting the most important words first
- Be precise – only use names of people, places or things
- If you want to find words that go together, put quote marks around them, for example 'ghost town' or 'bell witch'
- Use the advanced section of your search engine.

WHERE TO SEARCH

SEARCH ENGINE

A search engine looks through the entire web and lists all the sites that match your keywords. It can give thousands of links, but the best matches are at the top of the list, on the first page. Try **bbc.co.uk/search**

SEARCH DIRECTORY

A search directory is more like a library of websites. You can search by keyword or subject and browse through the different sites like you would look through books on a shelf. A good example is **yahooligans.com**

53

GLOSSARY

afterlife life after death

ancient from a past age long ago

bleak bare, cold and windy

blizzard bad snowstorm

brick up to close or block with bricks

coach house building where carriages were kept

con to fool, trick and generally 'take-in'

convent home for nuns

convict to find guilty of a crime and send to prison

creek stream

death row section of a prison for people sentenced to death

despair complete loss of hope

distinct unmistakable

disturb to break the calm and quiet

dungeon dark underground cell for locking up prisoners

eerie weird and frightening

effect something that happens as the result of an event or encounter

encounter unexpected meeting

evidence information available to help prove if something is true or false

execution carrying out the sentence of death

explanation reason that can be easily understood

floodlit to be lit up by large, powerful lights

footman servant

gas fumes harmful vapour from chemicals

gibbet pole for hanging criminals

heads of state leaders of different countries

helmsman sailor who steers a ship

hoax not real, a joke

hold-up robbery with a weapon

imprint stamp or impression

infrared the wavelength of light that allows a camera to 'see in the dark'

interfere to meddle and get in the way

investigate to search and study very carefully

jealous full of envy and hate of another person's success

jinxed brings bad luck

jury group of people in court who decide if a person is guilty

lantern lamp with a candle inside a glass case

legend story based on possible grains of truth

logbook where detailed records of events are written

lost soul sad ghost that cannot find rest after a miserable life

lurk to wait around, ready to strike

mansion very large house

orb shape of a ball or the globe

pantry walk-in food store

peer to look keenly but with some difficulty

phantom ghostly presence, something that is not real

plague deadly disease that spreads quickly

poltergeist noisy ghost that moves and drops objects

popular liked by many people

population all the people who live in a place or country

presence something very near

radiant glowing

rectory house of the vicar of the local church

re-enact to replay or repeat a performance

reflection image seen in a mirror

rehearsal practise for a performance

remote far away from other people

restore to repair and bring something back to its original state

revenge get even and pay someone back for wrongs done

right-angled 90° angle

scented has a pleasant smell

shriek shrill screech

sled sledge

superstitious believing in luck and the supernatural

tension mental strain and excitement

tragic sad and terrible, with an unhappy ending

trapdoor door in a floor, ceiling or roof

Tudor period in English history between 1485 and 1603

vault room for storing coffins

vicar priest in the Church of England

victim person who gets hurt or killed

wreckage smashed remains after a crash

INDEX